THIS BOOK IS FOR:

AND

BORN TO READ

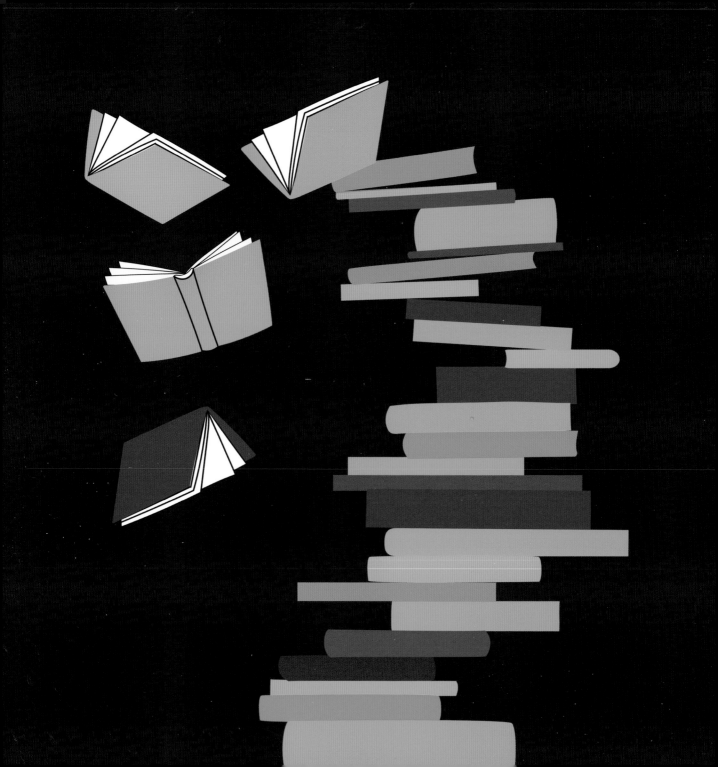

BORN TO READ

OUR FIRST FIVE YEARS IN BOOKS

A BOOK–A–DAY KEEPSAKE READING JOURNAL

L. J. TRACOSAS

GIRL FRIDAY BOOKS

 **GIRL FRIDAY BOOKS**

Published by Girl Friday Books™, Seattle

Produced by Girl Friday Productions
www.girlfridayproductions.com

Author: L. J. Tracosas
Design: Rachel Marek
Development & editorial: Emilie Sandoz-Voyer
Production editorial: Laura Dailey
Project management: Alexander Rigby

Image credits: All characters by Maria Starus
(except alligator by Kaliaha Volha); book illustrations
by Maria Starus, GoodStudio, Bibadash, and Lena
Nikolaeva; plaid pattern, ZillaDigital/Adobe Stock;
texture background, patternlibrary_nes/Shutterstock;
bookplate ribbon, Keep Calm and Vector/Shutterstock

ISBN: 978-1-7363579-4-1

Library of Congress Control Number: 2021906277

First edition
Printed in China

FOR MILES,
WHOSE HOPES AND DREAMS
WERE TO READ,
AND FOR NOLAN,
WHOSE STORY
IS JUST BEGINNING.

BORN TO READ

YOUR STORY BEGINS

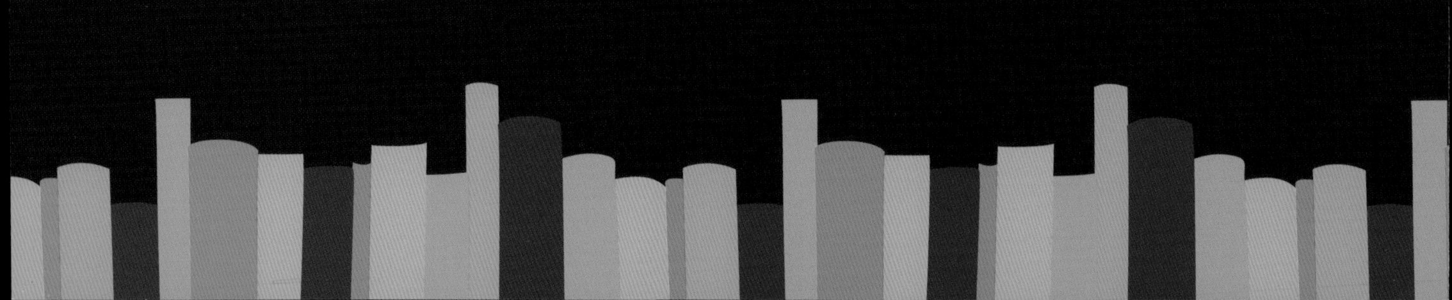

As your child begins their story, you and your family begin one of the most rewarding chapters in your life. Reading with your child every day is one important way to make sure this story is as rich and detailed as your favorite book.

Reading to children from birth to age five has bundles of benefits: it helps them develop language skills, encourages empathy and emotional development, fires up their imagination, helps them focus, and prepares them for school, especially in reading and writing. But most important, story time is quality time between you and your child.

ABOUT THIS BOOK

Born to Read is a keepsake memory book of your story time together and a guide to raising a reader, all rolled into one. Reading just one book a day for the first five years of your child's life will allow them to log almost two thousand books before kindergarten. In this book, you'll find the following:

- **Journal pages** where you can keep a list of the books you and your child read together from their birth to age five. It's a perfect way to recall particular favorites, record memories, and chronicle your child's reading journey—and when your child starts school, they will look back proudly at all the books they've logged.
- **Age-appropriate tips** for raising a reader and making the most of your story time together.
- **Book-recommendation lists** to help you expand your and your child's reading horizons and dive deeper into particular interest areas.
- **Your Child in Books sections**, where you can record specific reading milestones and passions and, as your child grows, interview them about the books they love.

- **Special Guest Story Time** sections, which allow extended family, friends, and visitors to record their recommendations and reflections on reading with your child.
- **Reading Reflections** sections, which let you look back on the previous year of books and write down memories for your child to revisit when they're older.
- **Resources** at the back of the book that offer more ways to broaden your child's reading experiences as they grow.

HOW TO USE THE JOURNAL PAGES

The first rule of *Born to Read* is: there are no rules! This book is a record for you and your child. It should reflect what you want it to reflect.

That said, here are some tips so you can make the most of the journal pages in this book *and* your time with your little bookworm:

- **Sit down to read with your child at least once a day.** The length of time depends on the time you have available and your child's attention span. Don't sweat it if you skip a day here and there.
- **Try to log at least one title a day.** Some days, you won't get through a book. Other days, you'll read a few in a row. That's totally fine. Log them all and watch your reading list grow and grow!
- **Yes, you can and should record the same book multiple times.** You'll find that your child becomes obsessed with certain titles, and reading the same book over and over not only soothes them but helps them learn more about words and stories. Recording those favorites in your reading log will allow you to look back and remember them. Every story time counts!

HAPPY READING!

AGE
0–1

ABOUT YOUR CHILD

The first year of your child's life is a burst of development. From birth, they are absorbing their environment through their senses, especially touch, taste, smell, and hearing. Their vision is also coming into focus. By three months, they start focusing and recognizing faces, reaching out, and babbling. By month six, they're developing motor skills, like grabbing, and becoming more curious about the world around them—and about themselves. Babies may recognize themselves in a mirror around this time. Around nine months, they're making all sorts of sounds, maybe even starting to respond to language and understand basic games like peekaboo.

Your baby may not focus on a book for most of their first year. So why read to your little one if they don't understand what you're saying or doing? Plenty of reasons. By the time your baby is one, they'll have heard many of the sounds they need to start speaking. The more they hear your voice—through reading and talking to them—the more sounds they'll absorb and the more ready they'll be. They also pick up on intonation, which can help them start to interpret emotion. Reading is also crucial bonding time between you and your little one, which is essential for development.

LOOK FOR BOOKS WITH . . .

- **Interactive elements.** Features like flaps, textures, and mirrors make a book a full sensory experience.
- **Simple language.** Single nouns, adjectives, verbs, numbers, colors, and letters are perfect for baby-sized attention spans.
- **Chewable pages!** Books are more than their contents for children at this age. They double as toys for tossing, tugging, and teething.

READING LOG

DATE	BOOK TITLE	NOTES

1. _____
2. _____
3. _____
4. _____
5. _____
6. _____
7. _____
8. _____
9. _____
10. _____
11. _____
12. _____
13. _____
14. _____
15. _____
16. _____

READ THROUGH THE RAINBOW

Books about color with high contrast
will catch your baby's eye.

Black on White by Tana Hoban

Bright Baby: Colors by Roger Priddy

Ellie in Color by Mike Wu

Look Look! by Peter Linenthal

Pantone: Colors by Pantone, illustrated by Helen Dardik

Red Rojo by Meritxell Martí, illustrated by Xavier Salomó

SQUARES, TRIANGLES, CIRCLES, OH MY!

Very basic shapes break the complex
world down into baby-sized bits.

Color Zoo by Lois Ehlert

My Very First Book of Shapes by Eric Carle

Perfect Square by Michael Hall

TouchThinkLearn: Shapes by Xavier Deneux

DATE	BOOK TITLE	NOTES
17.		
18.		
19.		
20.		
21.		
22.		
23.		
24.		
25.		
26.		
27.		
28.		
29.		
30.		

CATCH UP WHEN YOU'RE READY

In the first few weeks of your child's life, you're lucky if you can shower, let alone have it together enough for story time. We get it! Take your time and start logging when you're ready. In the meantime, talk to your little one as much as possible.

DATE	BOOK TITLE		NOTES

31. _____
32. _____
33. _____
34. _____
35. _____
36. _____
37. _____
38. _____
39. _____
40. _____
41. _____
42. _____
43. _____
44. _____
45. _____
46. _____
47. _____
48. _____
49. _____

DATE	BOOK TITLE	NOTES

50. ....
51. ....
52. ....
53. ....
54. ....
55. ....
56. ....
57. ....
58. ....
59. ....
60. ....
61. ....
62. ....
63. ....
64. ....
65. ....
66. ....
67. ....
68. ....

B IS FOR BOOK

Letters are the building blocks for learning to read.

Alphablock by Christopher Franceschelli, illustrated by Peskimo

Chicka Chicka Boom Boom by Bill Martin Jr. and John Archambault, illustrated by Lois Ehlert

Creature ABC by Andrew Zuckerman

Dr. Seuss's ABC: An Amazing Alphabet Book! by Dr. Seuss

LMNO Peas by Keith Baker

FUN WITH NUMBERS

Babies enjoy hearing anything repetitive and rhythmic, like counting.

1, 2, 3, Animals!: A First Counting Book for Toddlers by Bethany Lake

10 Little Rubber Ducks by Eric Carle

Babies Love Numbers by Scarlett Wing, illustrated by Anna Clark and Daniel Clark

Counting Kisses: A Kiss & Read Book by Karen Katz

Stack the Cats by Susie Ghahremani

DATE	BOOK TITLE	NOTES
69.		
70.		
71.		
72.		
73.		
74.		
75.		
76.		
77.		
78.		
79.		
80.		
81.		
82.		

BORED OF READING BOARD BOOKS?

Read your little one the newspaper, a grown-up book, or even today's tweets. The important thing for babies at this age is to hear words and your voice. Comprehending content comes later.

DATE	BOOK TITLE		NOTES

83.

84.

85.

86.

87.

88.

89.

90.

91.

92.

93.

94.

95.

96.

97.

98.

99.

100.

101.

Your personality is: _____

_____

Your favorite activities are: _____

_____

Reading with you is: _____

_____

The times of day that we read together are: _____

_____

You seem most interested in books that are about or feature:

• _____   • _____

• _____   • _____

• _____   • _____

The book we return to again and again is:

_____

I think you like this book because: _____

_____

My favorite books to read to you are . . .

Title   Because

_____

_____

_____

DATE	BOOK TITLE	NOTES
102.		
103.		
104.		
105.		
106.		
107.		
108.		
109.		
110.		
111.		
112.		
113.		
114.		
115.		
116.		
117.		
118.		
119.		
120.		

DATE	BOOK TITLE	NOTES

121. _____

122. _____

123. _____

124. _____

125. _____

126. _____

127. _____

128. _____

129. _____

130. _____

131. _____

132. _____

133. _____

134. _____

135. _____

136. _____

137. _____

138. _____

139. _____

SPECIAL GUEST STORY TIME!

Reader's name: _____

Relationship to you: _____

Date: _____ Location: _____

Reason for visit: _____
_____

We read these books together:
- _____ - _____
- _____ - _____
- _____ - _____

My favorite thing about reading with you is:
_____
_____

The book I liked reading to you the most was . . .
Title   *Because*
_____
_____
_____

Here are some reading suggestions from me to you: _____
_____
_____
_____

FACES AND FEELINGS

There's nothing more fascinating to
a baby than other baby faces!

Global Babies by the Global
Fund for Children

*Happy Face Sad Face: All Kinds
of Child Faces!* by Bill Cotter

I Love You, Elephant by Carles Ballesteros

*Making Faces: A First Book of
Emotions* by Abrams Appleseed

Mirror & Me: Feelings by Rose Colombe,
illustrated by Charlotte Pepper

Peekaboo Morning
by Rachel Isadora

DATE	BOOK TITLE	NOTES
140.		
141.		
142.		
143.		
144.		
145.		
146.		
147.		
148.		
149.		
150.		
151.		
152.		
153.		
154.		
155.		
156.		
157.		
158.		

DATE	BOOK TITLE	NOTES

159.
160.
161.
162.
163.
164.
165.
166.
167.
168.
169.
170.
171.
172.
173.
174.
175.
176.
177.

AND THE DUCK SAYS . . .

Babies love animals in real life and in books.

Hello, Ocean Friends: A High-Contrast Book by
Duopress Labs, illustrated by Violet Lemay

Indestructibles: Baby Animals created by
Amy Pixton, illustrated by Stephan Lomp

Sweetest Kulu by Celina Kalluk,
illustrated by Alexandria Neonakis

Tails by Matthew Van Fleet

VOCABULARY BUILDERS

It's never too early to start
connecting words to reading.

*Eating the Alphabet: Fruits and Vegetables
from A to Z* by Lois Ehlert

First 100 Words in English and Spanish by
Lil' Libros, illustrated by Ana Godinez

My First 101 Animals by Simon Abbott

My Very First Book of Words by Eric Carle

DATE	BOOK TITLE	NOTES
178.		
179.		
180.		
181.		
182.		
183.		
184.		
185.		
186.		
187.		
188.		
189.		
190.		

IT'S OK TO PLAY

Is your little one feeling squirmy? Not interested in turning the pages in order? Can't finish the book? Don't worry. It's okay to turn reading time into playtime at this age. Flip around in the book. Be silly. Ask questions. Make noises. Together time is the most important part.

DATE	BOOK TITLE	NOTES

191. _____

192. _____

193. _____

194. _____

195. _____

196. _____

197. _____

198. _____

199. _____

200. _____

201. _____

202. _____

203. _____

204. _____

205. _____

206. _____

207. _____

208. _____

209. _____

Your personality is: _____

_____

Your favorite activities are: _____

_____

Reading with you is: _____

_____

The times of day that we read together are: _____

_____

You like books that are about or feature:

• _____   • _____

• _____   • _____

• _____   • _____

The book we return to again and again is:

_____

I think you like this book because: _____

_____

My favorite books to read to you are . . .

Title   *Because*

_____

_____

_____

DATE	BOOK TITLE	NOTES

210.
211.
212.
213.
214.
215.
216.
217.
218.
219.
220.
221.
222.
223.
224.
225.
226.
227.
228.

DATE	BOOK TITLE	NOTES

229.
230.
231.
232.
233.
234.
235.
236.
237.
238.
239.
240.
241.
242.
243.
244.
245.
246.
247.

DATE	BOOK TITLE	NOTES
248.		
249.		
250.		
251.		
252.		
253.		
254.		
255.		
256.		
257.		
258.		
259.		
260.		
261.		

YOUR TURN

As your little one's motor skills increase and as they get familiar with the routine of story time, let them turn pages or reach for books off the shelf. Learning to interact with books—and you—is part of the fun.

WE ARE FAMILY

Right now, family is the center
of your kiddo's universe.

Auntie Loves You! by Helen Foster
James and Petra Brown

Besos for Baby: A Little Book of Kisses by
Jen Arena, illustrated by Blanca Gomez

Bunny Roo, I Love You by Melissa
Marr, illustrated by Teagan White

Homemade Love by bell hooks,
illustrated by Shane W. Evans

Love Makes a Family by Sophie Beer

My Two Dads and Me by Michael
Joosten, illustrated by Izak Zenou

My Two Moms and Me by Michael Joosten,
illustrated by Izak Zenou

The Family Book by Todd Parr

*We Belong Together: A Book
About Adoption and
Families* by Todd Parr

DATE	BOOK TITLE	NOTES
262.		
263.		
264.		
265.		
266.		
267.		
268.		
269.		
270.		
271.		
272.		
273.		
274.		
275.		
276.		
277.		
278.		
279.		
280.		

DATE	BOOK TITLE	NOTES

281.

282.

283.

284.

285.

286.

287.

288.

289.

290.

291.

292.

293.

294.

295.

296.

297.

298.

299.

SPECIAL GUEST STORY TIME!

Reader's name: _____

Relationship to you: _____

Date: _____ Location: _____

Reason for visit: _____
_____

We read these books together:

• _____ • _____
• _____ • _____
• _____ • _____

My favorite thing about reading with you is:
_____
_____

The book I liked reading to you the most was . . .

Title   *Because*
_____
_____

Here are some reading suggestions from me to you:
_____
_____
_____

DATE	BOOK TITLE	NOTES
300.		
301.		
302.		
303.		
304.		
305.		
306.		
307.		
308.		
309.		
310.		
311.		
312.		
313.		
314.		

THE PLOT THICKENS

Some babies at this age do gravitate toward board books with simple stories and a few sentences per page. Give it a try! For tips, see "Simple Storybooks" in the Age 1–2 section.

DATE	BOOK TITLE	NOTES

315. _____
316. _____
317. _____
318. _____
319. _____
320. _____
321. _____
322. _____
323. _____
324. _____
325. _____
326. _____
327. _____
328. _____
329. _____
330. _____
331. _____
332. _____
333. _____

DATE	BOOK TITLE		NOTES
334.			
335.			
336.			
337.			
338.			
339.			
340.			
341.			
342.			
343.			
344.			
345.			
346.			
347.			
348.			
349.			
350.			
351.			
352.			

DATE	BOOK TITLE	NOTES
353.		
354.		
355.		
356.		
357.		
358.		
359.		
360.		
361.		
362.		
363.		
364.		
365.		

WHAT WE'RE READING NEXT

Your personality is: _____

_____

Your favorite activities are: _____

_____

Reading with you is: _____

_____

The times of day that we read together are: _____

_____

You like books that are about or feature:

• _____   • _____

• _____   • _____

• _____   • _____

The book we return to again and again is:

_____

I think you like this book because: _____

_____

My favorite books to read to you are . . .

Title   *Because*

_____

_____

READING REFLECTIONS

Look back on the books you've logged this year and reflect on your time together.
Then answer these questions:

The books we read the most this year were: _____
_____
_____

I've noticed you grow in these ways during our reading time together this year: _____
_____
_____

I'll cherish this memory from reading with you this year: _____
_____
_____

Use this space to collect any other thoughts on your reading this year: _____
_____
_____
_____
_____
_____
_____

AGE
1-2

ABOUT YOUR CHILD

This year, your baby becomes a toddler. It's all about movement: walking, mimicking actions—maybe even dancing, and using things like forks, spoons, and brushes the right way. But it's also about finding their place in the world: they might eye strangers nervously or cry when you leave the room, but they'll also learn how to get your attention and how to follow requests and make them.

Communication skills are flourishing during this time. You'll hear first words, if you haven't already, and eventually back-to-back sentences. Your little one will love anything interactive—including story time! Let them pick the books you'll read. Have them help you turn pages. Stop between repeated lines in a book to see if they'll chime in. Ask them to act out movement in a story.

Sometimes it might feel like your toddler has less focus for books than they did when they were a baby (and it might be true!). Don't worry. Keep your story time together focused for as long as you can, but when your wiggle worm is done with sitting still, let them take the lead and have fun with it.

LOOK FOR BOOKS . . .

- **That have more sentences and easy story lines.** Your toddler is able to focus on books with one or two sentences per page and simple plots.
- **That have become your child's favorites.** By now, your child finds your reading habit comforting. You'll find they hone in on a few books that they like to return to night after night. Let them—and log them here as separate entries each time you read!
- **With opportunities to perform!** Add some flair to your read-aloud sessions. Be silly! Act out sentences! Make animal noises! Your audience will go wild.

READING LOG

| DATE | BOOK TITLE | NOTES |

1. _____
2. _____
3. _____
4. _____
5. _____
6. _____
7. _____
8. _____
9. _____
10. _____
11. _____
12. _____
13. _____
14. _____
15. _____
16. _____

DATE	BOOK TITLE		NOTES

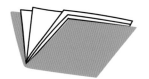

17.

18.

19.

20.

21.

22.

23.

24.

25.

26.

27.

28.

29.

30.

LET THEM PICK

Allow your little one to choose the books you read. They might surprise you—or you might read the same book you've read every night for a week. Either way, your toddler will love calling the shots!

DATE	BOOK TITLE		NOTES
31.			
32.			
33.			
34.			
35.			
36.			
37.			
38.			
39.			
40.			
41.			
42.			
43.			
44.			
45.			
46.			
47.			
48.			
49.			

BOOKS BECAUSE YOUR BABY CAN CHANGE THE WORLD

Inspire them early!

Antiracist Baby by Ibram X. Kendi, illustrated by Ashley Lukashevsky

Dream Big, Little One by Vashti Harrison

Little Feminist Board Book Set by Emily Kleinman, illustrated by Lydia Ortiz

Woke Baby by Mahogany L. Browne, illustrated by Theodore Taylor III

DATE	BOOK TITLE		NOTES
50.			
51.			
52.			
53.			
54.			
55.			
56.			
57.			
58.			
59.			
60.			
61.			
62.			
63.			

STICK WITH BOARD BOOKS

Your child might not be chewing on books as much as they did in the early days, but the durability of board books makes them a good choice for more powerful toddler hands.

DATE	BOOK TITLE	NOTES

64. _____

65. _____

66. _____

67. _____

68. _____

69. _____

70. _____

71. _____

72. _____

73. _____

74. _____

75. _____

76. _____

77. _____

78. _____

79. _____

80. _____

81. _____

82. _____

DATE	BOOK TITLE		NOTES

83.
84.
85.
86.
87.
88.
89.
90.
91.
92.
93.
94.
95.
96.
97.
98.
99.
100.
101.

STEM 101

Welcome to Baby U!

ABCs of Engineering by Chris Ferrie and Dr. Sara Kaiser

Baby 101: Architecture for Babies by Jonathan Litton, illustrated by Thomas Elliott

Baby Botanist by Dr. Laura Gehl, illustrated by Daniel Wiseman

Baby Loves Green Energy! by Ruth Spiro, illustrated by Irene Chan

Bathtime Mathtime by Danica McKellar, illustrated by Alicia Padrón

Nerdy Babies: Space by Emmy Kastner

Quantum Physics for Babies by Chris Ferrie

SPECIAL GUEST STORY TIME!

Reader's name: _____

Relationship to you: _____

Date: _____ Location: _____

Reason for visit: _____
_____

We read these books together:
- _____ - _____
- _____ - _____
- _____ - _____

My favorite thing about reading with you is:
_____
_____

The book I liked reading to you the most was . . .
Title   *Because*
_____
_____
_____

Here are some reading suggestions from me to you: _____
_____
_____
_____

DATE	BOOK TITLE	NOTES

102.

103.

104.

105.

106.

107.

108.

109.

110.

111.

112.

113.

114.

115.

116.

117.

118.

119.

120.

DATE	BOOK TITLE		NOTES
121.			
122.			
123.			
124.			
125.			
126.			
127.			
128.			
129.			
130.			
131.			
132.			
133.			
134.			
135.			
136.			
137.			
138.			
139.			

CAN'T-MISS CLASSICS FOR BABIES

You'll have these books memorized in no time!

Brown Bear, Brown Bear, What Do You See?
by Bill Martin Jr. and Eric Carle

Goodnight Moon by Margaret Wise Brown and Clement Hurd

On the Night You Were Born by Nancy Tillman

The Very Hungry Caterpillar by Eric Carle

Where's Spot? by Eric Hill

BOARD BOOKS OF GROWN-UP CLASSICS

Hook 'em while they're young!

Alice's Adventures in Wonderland by Lewis
Carroll, illustrated by Carly Gledhill

Cozy Classics: War & Peace by Jack Wang and Holman Wang

Little Master Shakespeare: Romeo & Juliet by
Jennifer Adams, illustrated by Alison Oliver

Pride & Prejudice: A BabyLit Counting Primer by
Jennifer Adams, illustrated by Alison Oliver

DATE	BOOK TITLE	NOTES
140.		
141.		
142.		
143.		
144.		
145.		
146.		
147.		
148.		
149.		
150.		
151.		
152.		

"WHAT DOES THE FOX SAY?"

Make reading an interactive experience by pausing to talk about the illustrations before you turn the page. Ask them to find something in the picture or elaborate on something in the image (for example, "Can you find the dog in this picture?" or "What does a dog say?").

DATE	BOOK TITLE	NOTES

153.
154.
155.
156.
157.
158.
159.
160.
161.
162.
163.
164.
165.
166.
167.
168.
169.
170.
171.

INTERACTIVE BOARD BOOKS

Books your baby can read,
feel, flip, flap, and pat.

Dear Zoo by Rod Campbell

Fuzzy Fuzzy Fuzzy! by Sandra Boynton

Pat the Bunny by Dorothy Kunhardt

Peek-a Who? by Nina Laden

See, Touch, Feel by Roger Priddy

Where Is Baby's Belly Button?
by Karen Katz

DATE	BOOK TITLE	NOTES

172. _____
173. _____
174. _____
175. _____
176. _____
177. _____
178. _____
179. _____
180. _____
181. _____
182. _____
183. _____
184. _____
185. _____
186. _____
187. _____
188. _____
189. _____
190. _____

Your personality is: _____

_____

Your favorite activities are: _____

_____

Reading with you is: _____

_____

The times of day that we read together are: _____

_____

You like books that are about or feature:

• _____   • _____

• _____   • _____

• _____   • _____

The book we return to again and again is:

_____

I think you like this book because: _____

_____

My favorite books to read to you are . . .

Title   Because

_____

_____

_____

DATE	BOOK TITLE	NOTES

191.
192.
193.
194.
195.
196.
197.
198.
199.
200.
201.
202.
203.
204.
205.
206.
207.
208.
209.

DATE	BOOK TITLE	NOTES

210.

211.

212.

213.

214.

215.

216.

217.

218.

219.

220.

221.

222.

223.

224.

225.

226.

227.

228.

SIMPLE STORYBOOKS

A good fit for your tot's attention span.

*Don't Let the Pigeon Drive
the Bus!* by Mo Willems

Giraffes Can't Dance by Giles Andreae,
illustrated by Guy Parker-Rees

Hug Machine by Scott Campbell

I Like Myself! by Karen Beaumont,
illustrated by David Catrow

Little Blue Truck by Alice Schertle,
illustrated by Jill McElmurry

Lola at the Library by Anna McQuinn,
illustrated by Rosalind Beardshaw

Sheep in a Jeep by Nancy Shaw,
illustrated by Margot Apple

*The Many Colors of
Harpreet Singh* by Supriya Kelkar,
illustrated by Alea Marley

DATE	BOOK TITLE	NOTES
229.		
230.		
231.		
232.		
233.		
234.		
235.		
236.		
237.		
238.		
239.		
240.		
241.		
242.		
243.		
244.		
245.		
246.		
247.		

DATE	BOOK TITLE		NOTES

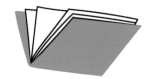

248.
249.
250.
251.
252.
253.
254.
255.
256.
257.
258.
259.
260.

SQUIRREL!

You might find your busy toddler too distracted to sit still for a whole story or multiple stories. That's OK! These energetic little wiggle worms are all about experiencing the world around them and moving their bodies. Experiment with different stories at different times of the day and see what works. Keep reading while they move about. You can also invite them to act out the story while you read.

Reader's name: _____

Relationship to you: _____

Date: _____ Location: _____

Reason for visit: _____
_____

We read these books together:

- _____   • _____
- _____   • _____
- _____   • _____

My favorite thing about reading with you is:
_____
_____

The book I liked reading to you the most was . . .
Title   *Because*
_____
_____
_____

Here are some reading suggestions from me to you: _____
_____
_____
_____

DATE	BOOK TITLE	NOTES

261.

262.

263.

264.

265.

266.

267.

268.

269.

270.

271.

272.

273.

274.

275.

276.

277.

278.

279.

DATE	BOOK TITLE		NOTES
280.			
281.			
282.			
283.			
284.			
285.			
286.			
287.			
288.			
289.			
290.			
291.			
292.			
293.			
294.			
295.			
296.			
297.			
298.			

DATE	BOOK TITLE		NOTES
299.			
300.			
301.			
302.			
303.			
304.			
305.			
306.			
307.			
308.			
309.			
310.			
311.			
312.			
313.			
314.			
315.			
316.			
317.			

BATH-TIME BOARD BOOKS FOR RUB-A-DUB-DUBS
Take story time to the tub!

Bath, Bath, Bath by Douglas Florian, illustrated by Christiane Engel

Splish, Splash, Baby! by Karen Katz

Tugga-Tugga Tugboat by Kevin Lewis, illustrated by Daniel Kirk

When Your Lion Needs a Bath by Susanna Leonard Hill, illustrated by Daniel Wiseman

BEDTIME STORIES FOR SWEET DREAMS
Snuggle up before bed.

A Book of Sleep by Il Sung Na

Bedtime, Ted! by Sophy Henn

Good Night Baby by Cheryl Willis Hudson, illustrated by George Ford

Llama Llama Red Pajama by Anna Dewdney

The Going to Bed Book by Sandra Boynton

The Goodnight Train by June Sobel, illustrated by Laura Huliska-Beith

Time for Bed by Mem Fox, illustrated by Jane Dyer

DATE	BOOK TITLE	NOTES
318.		
319.		
320.		
321.		
322.		
323.		
324.		
325.		
326.		
327.		
328.		
329.		
330.		
331.		
332.		
333.		
334.		
335.		
336.		

DATE	BOOK TITLE	NOTES

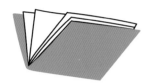

337.
338.
339.
340.
341.
342.
343.
344.
345.
346.
347.
348.
349.
350.
351.

SLOW DOWN

Take a moment to really listen to yourself while you read to your child. How's your pace? Reading more slowly will help your toddler understand the story.

DATE	BOOK TITLE	NOTES

352. _____
353. _____
354. _____
355. _____
356. _____
357. _____
358. _____
359. _____
360. _____
361. _____
362. _____
363. _____
364. _____
365. _____

WHAT WE'RE READING NEXT

Your personality is: _____

_____

Your favorite activities are: _____

_____

Reading with you is: _____

_____

The times of day that we read together are: _____

_____

You like books that are about or feature:

- _____   • _____
- _____   • _____
- _____   • _____

The book that fascinates you and we return to again and again is:

_____

I think you like this book because: _____

_____

My favorite books to read to you are . . .

Title   *Because*

_____

_____

_____

READING REFLECTIONS

Look back on the books you've logged this year and reflect on your time together.
Then answer these questions:

The books we read the most were: _____
_____
_____
_____

I've noticed you grow in these ways during our reading time together: _____
_____
_____

I'll cherish this memory from reading with you: _____
_____
_____

Use this space to collect any other thoughts on your reading this year: _____
_____
_____
_____
_____
_____
_____
_____

AGE
2-3

ABOUT YOUR CHILD

Hello, Mr. or Ms. Independent! As your toddler becomes a threenager, you might experience your share of tantrums. But you'll also see your tot turning into a big(ger) kid. They're making large leaps in development this year. They're learning to play with other kids in groups—and all the things that go with that! They're having big emotions, but they're also learning to self-soothe. They're getting more coordinated in their movements, like throwing and catching, running and jumping.

They're understanding and being understood more. Over the course of this year, they'll start using prepositions and plurals, and they'll talk in sentences rather than phrases. They'll also start asking the perennial kid question: Why?

Your little one will love stories with more words and more involved plots. And they'll start to pull context clues from pictures about what's happening. They'll also start to empathize with characters and think about what happens next.

LOOK FOR BOOKS . . .

- **That reflect their interests.** Dinosaur obsessed? Foodie in the making? Wild for horses? Feed their interests.
- **That reflect the world around them and the things they do.** For example, think books about trucks, grocery shopping, going to the doctor, or bedtime routines.
- **With regular pages.** You might still want to watch an enthusiastic page-turner closely, but you can start shelving those board books.

READING LOG

DATE	BOOK TITLE	NOTES

1. _____
2. _____
3. _____
4. _____
5. _____
6. _____
7. _____
8. _____
9. _____
10. _____
11. _____
12. _____
13. _____
14. _____
15. _____
16. _____

DATE	BOOK TITLE		NOTES

17. _____

18. _____

19. _____

20. _____

21. _____

22. _____

23. _____

24. _____

25. _____

26. _____

27. _____

28. _____

29. _____

30. _____

STORY (ANY)TIME

Out running errands but don't have a book? Make up a story and tell it to your child as you go. Make them the main character. This trick can work anytime to keep your kid's mind occupied—and you're building communication skills while you're at it!

NOM, NOM, NOM

Encourage adventurous eating with
these books about food.

Can I Eat That? by Joshua David Stein,
illustrated by Julia Rothman

Dragons Love Tacos by Adam Rubin,
illustrated by Daniel Salmieri

Fry Bread: A Native American Family Story by Kevin
Noble Maillard, illustrated by Juana Martinez-Neal

Full, Full, Full of Love by Trish Cooke,
illustrated by Paul Howard

Little Pea by Amy Krouse Rosenthal,
illustrated by Jen Corace

Peanut Butter and Cupcake by Terry Border

Stir Crack Whisk Bake by America's Test
Kitchen Kids and Maddie Frost

The Ugly Vegetables by Grace Lin

What Can You Do with a Paleta? by
Carmen Tafolla, illustrated by Magaly Morales

DATE	BOOK TITLE	NOTES

31. _____

32. _____

33. _____

34. _____

35. _____

36. _____

37. _____

38. _____

39. _____

40. _____

41. _____

42. _____

43. _____

44. _____

45. _____

46. _____

47. _____

48. _____

49. _____

DATE	BOOK TITLE		NOTES
50.			
51.			
52.			
53.			
54.			
55.			
56.			
57.			
58.			
59.			
60.			
61.			
62.			
63.			
64.			
65.			
66.			
67.			
68.			

DATE	BOOK TITLE	NOTES
69.		
70.		
71.		
72.		
73.		
74.		
75.		
76.		
77.		
78.		
79.		
80.		
81.		
82.		

RELATE TO THEM

Pick out elements of the book that your child can identify with, and talk about them. If the story is about bath time, ask them to tell you about theirs. Does the main character live in the city like you do? Ask your child what things in the book they also see in their city.

BUST A RHYME

With these books that rhyme,
you'll both love story time.

Each Peach Pear Plum by Janet
Ahlberg and Allan Ahlberg

Hush: A Thai Lullaby by Minfong Ho,
illustrated by Holly Meade

I Know a Lot! by Stephen Krensky,
illustrated by Sara Gillingham

Jamberry by Bruce Degen

Little You by Richard Van Camp, illustrated by Julie Flett

Madeline by Ludwig Bemelmans

*Rap a Tap Tap: Here's Bojangles—Think of
That!* by Diane Dillon and Leo Dillon

The Thing About Bees: A Love Letter by Shabazz Larkin

They, She, He, Easy as ABC by Maya
Christina Gonzalez and Matthew SG

Wild About Books by Judy Sierra,
illustrated by Marc Brown

DATE	BOOK TITLE		NOTES

83.
84.
85.
86.
87.
88.
89.
90.
91.
92.
93.
94.
95.
96.
97.
98.
99.
100.
101.

DATE	BOOK TITLE	NOTES
102.		
103.		
104.		
105.		
106.		
107.		
108.		
109.		
110.		
111.		
112.		
113.		
114.		
115.		
116.		
117.		
118.		
119.		
120.		

Reader's name: _____

Relationship to you: _____

Date: _____ Location: _____

Reason for visit: _____

_____

We read these books together:

- _____ • _____
- _____ • _____
- _____ • _____

My favorite thing about reading with you is:

_____

_____

The book I liked reading to you the most was . . .

Title   *Because*

_____

_____

_____

Here are some reading suggestions from me to you: _____

_____

_____

_____

DATE	BOOK TITLE	NOTES
121.		
122.		
123.		
124.		
125.		
126.		
127.		
128.		
129.		
130.		
131.		
132.		
133.		
134.		
135.		
136.		
137.		
138.		
139.		

DATE	BOOK TITLE	NOTES

140. _____
141. _____
142. _____
143. _____
144. _____
145. _____
146. _____
147. _____
148. _____
149. _____
150. _____
151. _____
152. _____
153. _____

READ AND REPEAT

Have you read your tot's favorite book so many times, you have it memorized? They probably do too. Have them help out by letting them finish sentences or rhymes that they know by heart, or let them tell you what's coming up in the story.

DATE	BOOK TITLE	NOTES
154.		
155.		
156.		
157.		
158.		
159.		
160.		
161.		
162.		
163.		
164.		
165.		
166.		
167.		
168.		
169.		
170.		
171.		
172.		

Your personality is: _____

_____

Your favorite activities are: _____

_____

Reading with you is: _____

_____

The times of day that we read together are: _____

_____

You like books that are about or feature:

• _____   • _____

• _____   • _____

• _____   • _____

The book we return to again and again is:

_____

I think you like this book because: _____

_____

My favorite books to read to you are . . .

Title   *Because*

_____   _____

_____   _____

_____   _____

DATE	BOOK TITLE		NOTES
173.			
174.			
175.			
176.			
177.			
178.			
179.			
180.			
181.			
182.			
183.			
184.			
185.			
186.			
187.			
188.			
189.			
190.			
191.			

FAVORITE TODDLER TOPICS

Chances are your little one is getting into at least one of these perennial favorite kid topics.

TRUCKS

Alphabet Trucks by Samantha R. Vamos, illustrated by Ryan O'Rourke

Goodnight, Goodnight, Construction Site by Sherri Duskey Rinker, illustrated by Tom Lichtenheld

Richard Scarry's Cars and Trucks from A to Z by Richard Scarry

HORSES

Noni the Pony by Alison Lester

Robert the Rose Horse by Joan Heilbroner, illustrated by P. D. Eastman

SPACE

Look, There's a Rocket! by Esther Aarts

Swift Walker: A Space Adventure by Verlyn Tarlton, illustrated by Ravshan Karimov

ON THE FARM

Big Red Barn by Margaret Wise Brown,
illustrated by Felicia Bond

Night Night Farm by Roger Priddy

Barnyard Dance! by Sandra Boynton

TRAINS

Freight Train by Donald Crews

Trains Coming Through! by Stephanie
Morgan, illustrated by Joe Bucco

DANCE

Boys Dance! by John Robert Allman,
illustrated by Luciano Lozano

How Do You Dance? by Thyra Heder

DINOSAURS

If the Dinosaurs Came Back
by Bernard Most

Tadpole Rex by Kurt Cyrus

DATE	BOOK TITLE		NOTES
192.			
193.			
194.			
195.			
196.			
197.			
198.			
199.			
200.			
201.			
202.			
203.			
204.			
205.			
206.			
207.			
208.			
209.			
210.			

DATE	BOOK TITLE	NOTES

211.

212.

213.

214.

215.

216.

217.

218.

219.

220.

221.

222.

223.

224.

225.

226.

227.

228.

229.

DATE	BOOK TITLE	NOTES
230.		
231.		
232.		
233.		
234.		
235.		
236.		
237.		
238.		
239.		
240.		
241.		
242.		
243.		
244.		

BEDTIME STORIES AND BREAKFAST STORIES

Story time can be anytime! If your tired tot isn't up for books at the end of the day, try reading over breakfast, before naps, or whenever works for you and your kiddo.

SPECIAL GUEST STORY TIME!

Reader's name: _____

Relationship to you: _____

Date: _____ Location: _____

Reason for visit: _____
_____

We read these books together:

- _____ • _____
- _____ • _____
- _____ • _____

My favorite thing about reading with you is:
_____
_____

The book I liked reading to you the most was . . .

Title   *Because*
_____
_____
_____

Here are some reading suggestions from me to you: _____
_____
_____
_____

DATE	BOOK TITLE	NOTES

245.
246.
247.
248.
249.
250.
251.
252.
253.
254.
255.
256.
257.
258.
259.
260.
261.
262.
263.

DATE	BOOK TITLE		NOTES

264.
265.
266.
267.
268.
269.
270.
271.
272.
273.
274.
275.
276.
277.
278.
279.
280.
281.
282.

DATE	BOOK TITLE	NOTES
283.		
284.		
285.		
286.		
287.		
288.		
289.		
290.		
291.		
292.		
293.		
294.		
295.		
296.		
297.		
298.		
299.		
300.		
301.		

DATE	BOOK TITLE		NOTES
302.			
303.			
304.			
305.			
306.			
307.			
308.			
309.			
310.			
311.			
312.			
313.			
314.			
315.			
316.			
317.			
318.			
319.			
320.			

DITCH THE DIAPERS!

In the throes of potty training? Or just feeling silly? Here are books about bathrooms and underpants.

Big Girl Panties by Fran Manushkin, illustrated by Valeria Petrone

Even Firefighters Go to the Potty by Wendy Wax and Naomi Wax, illustrated by Stephen Gilpin

Polar Bear's Underwear by Tupera Tupera

Potty by Leslie Patricelli

The Potty Train by David Hochman and Ruth Kennison, illustrated by Derek Anderson

Vegetables in Underwear by Jared Chapman

DATE	BOOK TITLE	NOTES
321.		
322.		
323.		
324.		
325.		
326.		
327.		
328.		
329.		
330.		
331.		
332.		
333.		
334.		
335.		
336.		
337.		
338.		
339.		

DATE	BOOK TITLE	NOTES
340.		
341.		
342.		
343.		
344.		
345.		
346.		
347.		
348.		
349.		
350.		
351.		
352.		
353.		
354.		

BELLS, WHISTLES, HONKS, AND TOOTS

Go beyond the page! Books with interactive elements like flaps, soundboards, tabs, puppets, and pop-ups will be a big hit.

DATE	BOOK TITLE	NOTES
355.		
356.		
357.		
358.		
359.		
360.		
361.		
362.		
363.		
364.		
365.		

WHAT WE'RE READING NEXT

Your personality is: _____

_____

Your favorite activities are: _____

_____

Reading with you is: _____

_____

The times of day that we read together are: _____

_____

You seem most interested in books that are about or feature:

- _____ - _____
- _____ - _____
- _____ - _____

The book we return to again and again is:

_____

I think you like this book because: _____

_____

My favorite books to read to you are . . .

Title   *Because*

_____

_____

_____

INTERVIEW YOUR CHILD!

Ask your child these questions and write down their answers word for word!

What's your favorite book? _____
_____
_____
_____

Why do you like it? _____
_____
_____
_____

If you could read a book about anything at all, what would it be? _____
_____
_____
_____
_____

What's your favorite part about reading books with me? _____
_____
_____
_____
_____

READING REFLECTIONS

Look back on the books you've logged this year and reflect on your time together.
Then answer these questions:

The books we read the most were: _____
_____
_____
_____

I've noticed you grow in these ways during our reading time together: _____
_____
_____
_____

I'll cherish this memory from reading with you: _____
_____
_____
_____

Use this space to collect any other thoughts on your reading this year: _____
_____
_____
_____
_____
_____
_____
_____
_____

AGE
3-4

ABOUT YOUR CHILD

Welcome to what some child development experts call "the magic years." You'll see your little one-turned-big kid's imagination bloom. Pretend play and storytelling are hallmarks of this age. And these happen alongside social and emotional milestones, like cooperation and negotiation with others, and physical ones, like balance and motor skills needed for throwing and kicking a ball.

Their language skills are expanding, too. You'll hear your little one using grammatically correct wording more and more, and you'll find yourself translating for them with strangers less and less. They're starting to recognize letters and letter sound. Ask "What letter does banana start with?" and they just might answer correctly.

All of this combines to give your three-going-on-four-year-old child a richly vibrant world that you can easily supplement with wonderful storybooks.

LOOK FOR BOOKS . . .

- **With more complex plots**—they'll be able to follow them.
- **With more complex nonfiction topics**— space, undersea exploration, time.
- **With fantasy worlds.** Fuel their imagination!
- **With three or four sentences per page.**

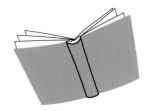

READING LOG

DATE	BOOK TITLE	NOTES

1.
2.
3.
4.
5.
6.
7.
8.
9.
10.
11.
12.
13.
14.
15.
16.

IMAGINATION INSPIRATION

These imaginative picture books will
inspire your child's creativity!

Boxitects by Kim Smith

Du Iz Tak? by Carson Ellis

Galimoto by Karen Lynn Williams,
illustrated by Catherine Stock

Hana Hashimoto Sixth Violin by Chieri Uegaki,
illustrated by Qin Leng

Izzy Gizmo by Pip Jones, illustrated by Sara Ogilvie

My Rainy Day Rocket Ship by Markette
Sheppard, illustrated by Charly Palmer

Squeak, Rumble, Whomp! Whomp! Whomp! by
Wynton Marsalis, illustrated by Paul Rogers

The Carpenter by Bruna Barros

The Old Truck by Jarrett Pumphrey and Jerome Pumphrey

They All Saw a Cat by Brendan Wenzel

What If . . . by Samantha Berger, illustrated by Mike Curato

When I Woke Up I Was a Hippopotamus by
Tom MacRae, illustrated by Ross Collins

DATE	BOOK TITLE		NOTES
17.			
18.			
19.			
20.			
21.			
22.			
23.			
24.			
25.			
26.			
27.			
28.			
29.			
30.			

HELP THEM MAKE WORDS THEIR OWN

If you come across a word your child might not know, define it for them with a synonym. Then help them use the new word in a sentence.

DATE	BOOK TITLE	NOTES
31.		
32.		
33.		
34.		
35.		
36.		
37.		
38.		
39.		
40.		
41.		
42.		
43.		
44.		
45.		
46.		
47.		
48.		
49.		

ROUSING TALES

Though they be little, they are mighty. Help your little one feel empowered with these books about positive protagonists.

Ambitious Girl by Meena Harris

At the Mountain's Base by Traci Sorell, illustrated by Weshoyot Alvitre

Carmin Cares by Karen Kilpatrick

City Green by DyAnne DiSalvo-Ryan

Drum Dream Girl by Margarita Engle, illustrated by Rafael López

Grace Goes to Washington by Kelly DiPucchio

I Am So Brave! by Stephen Krensky, illustrated by Sara Gillingham

I Can Do It Too! by Karen Baicker

Jabari Jumps by Gaia Cornwall

Riley Can Be Anything by Davina Hamilton, illustrated by Elena Reinoso

The Camping Trip by Jennifer K. Mann

When We Were Alone by David A. Robertson, illustrated by Julie Flett

DATE	BOOK TITLE	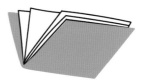	NOTES

50.

51.

52.

53.

54.

55.

56.

57.

58.

59.

60.

61.

62.

63.

64.

65.

66.

67.

68.

DATE	BOOK TITLE	NOTES
69.		
70.		
71.		
72.		
73.		
74.		
75.		
76.		
77.		
78.		
79.		
80.		
81.		
82.		
83.		
84.		
85.		
86.		
87.		

SPECIAL GUEST STORY TIME!

Reader's name: _____

Relationship to you: _____

Date: _____ Location: _____

Reason for visit: _____
_____

We read these books together:

• _____ • _____
• _____ • _____
• _____ • _____

My favorite thing about reading with you is:
_____
_____

The book I liked reading to you the most was . . .

Title *Because*
_____
_____
_____

Here are some reading suggestions from me to you: _____
_____
_____
_____

DATE	BOOK TITLE	NOTES
88.		
89.		
90.		
91.		
92.		
93.		
94.		
95.		
96.		
97.		
98.		
99.		
100.		
101.		

FOLLOW YOUR FINGERS

As you read, trace the text with your finger. This small habit will help set the stage for your child becoming a reader. They'll pick up that words go from left to right by following your movement, and they'll connect what they're hearing with what they're seeing.

DATE	BOOK TITLE	NOTES
102.		
103.		
104.		
105.		
106.		
107.		
108.		
109.		
110.		
111.		
112.		
113.		
114.		
115.		
116.		
117.		
118.		
119.		
120.		

EMOTIONS EVERY DAY

These books acknowledge that some days we
feel happy, some days we feel angry, and some days
we feel everything in between—and that's OK!

Grumpy Monkey by Suzanne Lang, illustrated by Max Lang

In My Heart: A Book of Feelings by Jo Witek,
illustrated by Christine Roussey

Monster Trouble by Lane Fredrickson,
illustrated by Michael Robertson

My Cold Plum Lemon Pie Bluesy Mood by Tameka
Fryer Brown, illustrated by Shane W. Evans

My Heart by Corinna Luyken

Ruby Finds a Worry by Tom Percival

The Boy with Big, Big Feelings by Britney
Winn Lee, illustrated by Jacob Souva

*Today I Feel Silly: And Other Moods That Make My
Day* by Jamie Lee Curtis, illustrated by Laura Cornell

DATE	BOOK TITLE	NOTES
121.		
122.		
123.		
124.		
125.		
126.		
127.		
128.		
129.		
130.		
131.		
132.		
133.		
134.		
135.		
136.		
137.		
138.		
139.		

DATE	BOOK TITLE	NOTES
140.		
141.		
142.		
143.		
144.		
145.		
146.		
147.		
148.		
149.		
150.		
151.		
152.		
153.		

YOUR LITTLE STORYTELLER

Weave story time into dinner by encouraging your kid to make up a tall tale. Get them started with a simple prompt: "One day, the cat put on his sneakers and went outside. And then . . ." Let your little one take over or take turns around the table.

DATE	BOOK TITLE		NOTES

154.
155.
156.
157.
158.
159.
160.
161.
162.
163.
164.
165.
166.
167.
168.
169.
170.
171.
172.

DATE	BOOK TITLE		NOTES

173. _____

174. _____

175. _____

176. _____

177. _____

178. _____

179. _____

180. _____

181. _____

182. _____

183. _____

184. _____

185. _____

186. _____

187. _____

188. _____

189. _____

190. _____

191. _____

YOUR CHILD IN BOOKS AT . . . 3 AND A HALF

Your personality is: _____

Your favorite activities are: _____

Reading with you is: _____

The times of day that we read together are: _____

You like books that are about or feature:

- _____   - _____
- _____   - _____
- _____   - _____

The book we return to again and again is: _____

I think you like this book because: _____

My favorite books to read to you are . . .

Title   *Because*

_____
_____
_____

BOOKS FOR ALL WEATHER

From thunderstorms and downpours to glittering snow and glorious rainbows, the weather is full of drama and beauty to inspire and delight your reading buddy.

A Rainbow of My Own by Don Freeman

All About Weather by Huda Harajli MA

Bear Feels Scared by Karma Wilson, illustrated by Jane Chapman

Franklin and the Thunderstorm by Paulette Bourgeois, illustrated by Brenda Clark

Haiku Baby by Betsy E. Snyder

No Two Alike by Keith Baker

Rain! by Linda Ashman, illustrated by Christian Robinson

Rain Before Rainbows by Smriti Prasadam-Halls, illustrated by David Litchfield

The Mitten by Jan Brett

DATE	BOOK TITLE	NOTES
192.		
193.		
194.		
195.		
196.		
197.		
198.		
199.		
200.		
201.		
202.		
203.		
204.		
205.		
206.		
207.		
208.		
209.		
210.		

DATE	BOOK TITLE		NOTES
211.			
212.			
213.			
214.			
215.			
216.			
217.			
218.			
219.			
220.			
221.			
222.			
223.			
224.			
225.			

MAKE IT UP

Let your child "read" the story. Let them pick up a new book and tell you the story, which they can invent based on the pictures and their imagination.

DATE	BOOK TITLE		NOTES

226. ....

227. ....

228. ....

229. ....

230. ....

231. ....

232. ....

233. ....

234. ....

235. ....

236. ....

237. ....

238. ....

239. ....

240. ....

241. ....

242. ....

243. ....

244. ....

TRUE STORIES

Let these biographical picture books
inspire your little one—and you!

Encounter by Brittany Luby, illustrated by Michaela Goade

*Go Show the World: A Celebration of Indigenous
Heroes* by Wab Kinew, illustrated by Joe Morse

*Henry's Freedom Box: A True Story from the Underground
Railroad* by Ellen Levine, illustrated by Kadir Nelson

Me . . . Jane by Patrick McDonnell

My Name is Celia: The Life of Celia Cruz by
Monica Brown, illustrated by Raphael López

*Shark Lady: The True Story of How Eugenie Clark
Became the Ocean's Most Fearless Scientist* by Jess
Keating, illustrated by Marta Álvarez Miguéns

*Sisters and Champions: The True Story of Venus and Serena
Williams* by Howard Bryant, illustrated by Floyd Cooper

*The Girl Who Thought in Pictures: The Story of Dr. Temple
Grandin* by Julia Finley Mosca, illustrated by Daniel Rieley

The People Shall Continue by Simon J.
Ortiz, illustrated by Sharol Graves

DATE	BOOK TITLE		NOTES

245. _____
246. _____
247. _____
248. _____
249. _____
250. _____
251. _____
252. _____
253. _____
254. _____
255. _____
256. _____
257. _____
258. _____
259. _____
260. _____
261. _____
262. _____
263. _____

	DATE	BOOK TITLE	NOTES
264.			
265.			
266.			
267.			
268.			
269.			
270.			
271.			
272.			
273.			
274.			
275.			
276.			
277.			
278.			
279.			
280.			
281.			
282.			

EXPANDING HORIZONS

Foster interest in world cultures during reading time.

Beautiful Moon by Tonya Bolden, illustrated by Eric Velasquez

Eight Days: A Story of Haiti by Edwidge
Danticat, illustrated by Alix Delinois

I Live in Tokyo by Mari Takabayashi

King for a Day by Rukhsana Khan, illustrated by Christiane Krömer

Mrs. Katz and Tush by Patricia Polacco

Round Is a Mooncake by Roseanne Thong, illustrated by Grace Lin

The Proudest Blue: A Story of Hijab and Family
by Ibtihaj Muhammad and S. K. Ali

The Sharing Circle, Stories About First Nations Culture
by Theresa Muese, illustrated by Arthur Stevens

Uncle Peter's Amazing Chinese Wedding by
Lenore Look, illustrated by Yumi Heo

Tai series by Marcel A. Bent

We Are Grateful: Otsaliheliga by Traci Sorell,
illustrated by Frané Lessac

DATE	BOOK TITLE	NOTES

283. _____

284. _____

285. _____

286. _____

287. _____

288. _____

289. _____

290. _____

291. _____

292. _____

293. _____

294. _____

295. _____

296. _____

GET TO KNOW THOSE ABCs

Use reading time as a way to prime your child's excitement for reading. Point out letters in the text and ask your kid if they can identify them and the sounds they make. Don't worry about wrong answers. Have fun with it!

DATE	BOOK TITLE	NOTES

297.
298.
299.
300.
301.
302.
303.
304.
305.
306.
307.
308.
309.
310.
311.
312.
313.
314.
315.

Reader's name: _____

Relationship to you: _____

Date: _____ Location: _____

Reason for visit: _____
_____

We read these books together:

- _____   • _____
- _____   • _____
- _____   • _____

My favorite thing about reading with you is:
_____
_____

The book I liked reading to you the most was . . .

Title   *Because*
_____
_____
_____

Here are some reading suggestions from me to you: _____
_____
_____
_____

DATE	BOOK TITLE	NOTES
316.		
317.		
318.		
319.		
320.		
321.		
322.		
323.		
324.		
325.		
326.		
327.		
328.		
329.		
330.		
331.		
332.		
333.		
334.		

CALDECOTT CLASSICS

These award-winning classics and destined-to-be classics will delight your budding reader.

Owl Moon by Jane Yolen, illustrated by John Schoenherr

The Lion & the Mouse by Jerry Pinkney

The Little House by Virginia Lee Burton

The Snowy Day by Ezra Jack Keats

This Is Not My Hat by Jon Klassen

We Are Water Protectors by Carole Lindstrom, illustrated by Michaela Goade

Where the Wild Things Are by Maurice Sendak

Wolf in the Snow by Matthew Cordell

DATE	BOOK TITLE	NOTES

335.

336.

337.

338.

339.

340.

341.

342.

343.

344.

345.

346.

347.

348.

349.

350.

351.

352.

353.

DATE	BOOK TITLE		NOTES
354.			
355.			
356.			
357.			
358.			
359.			
360.			
361.			
362.			
363.			
364.			
365.			

WHAT WE'RE READING NEXT

Your personality is: _____

_____

Your favorite activities are: _____

_____

Reading with you is: _____

_____

The times of day that we read together are: _____

_____

You seem most interested in books that are about or feature:

• _____   • _____

• _____   • _____

• _____   • _____

The book that fascinates you and we return to again and again is:

_____

I think you like this book because: _____

_____

My favorite books to read to you are . . .

Title   Because

_____

_____

_____

INTERVIEW YOUR CHILD!

Ask your child these questions and write down their answers word for word!

What are some of your favorite books we've read this year? _____
_____
_____
_____

Why do you like them? _____
_____
_____
_____

If you were a character in a book, what character would you be?
What would the book be about? _____
_____
_____
_____

What's your favorite part about reading books with me? _____
_____
_____
_____

READING REFLECTIONS

Look back on the books you've logged this year and reflect on your time together. Then answer these questions:

The books we read the most were: _____
_____
_____
_____

I've noticed you grow in these ways during our reading time together: _____
_____
_____
_____

I'll cherish this memory from reading with you: _____
_____
_____
_____

Use this space to collect any other thoughts on your reading this year: _____
_____
_____
_____
_____
_____
_____
_____

AGE
4—5

ABOUT YOUR CHILD

You've got a full-blown kid on your hands! This year, your child will become more independent: they'll brush their own teeth, dress themselves, and handle their bathroom business. They'll also count things and understand time, and generally they will grasp everyday concepts. They'll even start writing letters and drawing figures. They can be your biggest helper or your biggest roadblock around the house—they understand the rules and what needs to be done, and might have opinions about that!

Your child likely has a circle of friends now, and they probably amuse themselves just fine without any adult input whatsoever. Your little ham probably likes to sing and dance. They're still telling stories, but more complex ones now. Your child speaks in paragraphs now, not just sentences. This means they're ready for more complex books as well!

By this age, kids understand that written words tell stories. When you read with them, you might notice that they're engaged and like to talk about what you're reading more. They might also be able to recognize some words in the text or pictures. You are getting very close to having your own little reader!

LOOK FOR BOOKS . . .

- **That give you something to talk about.** Ask your child questions about what you're reading together. You'll love hearing their thoughts just as much as they'll love sharing.
- **That reflect your child's broadening interests.** Did they just join a soccer team? Are they dreaming of being a veterinarian? Find books on subjects that fascinate.
- **With reading stages.** Several publishers produce paperback series labeled with reading stages. Pick a few that you can read together, and encourage your early reader to try reading on their own.

READING LOG

DATE	BOOK TITLE	NOTES

1. _____
2. _____
3. _____
4. _____
5. _____
6. _____
7. _____
8. _____
9. _____
10. _____
11. _____
12. _____
13. _____
14. _____
15. _____
16. _____

DATE	BOOK TITLE	NOTES

17.

18.

19.

20.

21.

22.

23.

24.

25.

26.

27.

28.

29.

30.

31.

MIX IT UP

Make sure to read a variety of books together. Fiction and nonfiction, storybooks and comics, poetry and chapter books.

BOOKS FOR TOUGH TIMES

Children connect what they read in books with what they experience in life. And sometimes, life deals even the littlest ones a tough time. Here are some books that might help.

A Big Guy Took My Ball! by Mo Willems (bullying)

A Kiss Goodbye by Audrey Penn, illustrated by Barbara L. Gibson (moving)

Dinosaurs Divorce by Marc Brown, illustrated by Laurene Krasny Brown (divorce and separation)

Ida, Always by Caron Levis, illustrated by Charles Santoso (grief/loss)

Lenny & Lucy by Philip C. Stead, illustrated by Erin E. Stead (moving)

Purplicious by Elizabeth Kann, illustrated by Victoria Kann (bullying)

The River of Birds by Libby Moore, illustrated by Michael Boardman (grief/loss)

The Rough Patch by Brian Lies (grief/loss)

Two Homes by Claire Masurel, illustrated by Kady MacDonald Denton (divorce and separation)

DATE	BOOK TITLE	NOTES

32.
33.
34.
35.
36.
37.
38.
39.
40.
41.
42.
43.
44.
45.
46.
47.
48.
49.
50.

| DATE | BOOK TITLE |  | NOTES |

51. _____
52. _____
53. _____
54. _____
55. _____
56. _____
57. _____
58. _____
59. _____
60. _____
61. _____
62. _____
63. _____
64. _____
65. _____
66. _____
67. _____
68. _____
69. _____

DATE	BOOK TITLE	NOTES
70.		
71.		
72.		
73.		
74.		
75.		
76.		
77.		
78.		
79.		
80.		
81.		
82.		
83.		
84.		
85.		
86.		
87.		
88.		

BEST FRIENDS IN BOOKS

Friends are becoming more important to your kiddo, and they'll enjoy reading about other friendships.

A Sick Day for Amos McGee by Philip C. Stead, illustrated by Erin E. Stead

Bob and Otto by Robert O. Bruel, illustrated by Nick Bruel

Corduroy by Don Freeman

Frog and Toad Are Friends by Arnold Lobel

Mr. Prickles: A Quill-Fated Love Story by Karan LaReau, illustrated by Scott Magoon

The Adventures of Beekle: The Unimaginary Friend by Dan Santat

There Is a Bird on Your Head! by Mo Willems

You Are Friendly by Todd Snow, illustrated by Melodee Strong

DATE	BOOK TITLE	NOTES

89. _____

90. _____

91. _____

92. _____

93. _____

94. _____

95. _____

96. _____

97. _____

98. _____

99. _____

100. _____

101. _____

102. _____

103. _____

104. _____

105. _____

106. _____

107. _____

DATE	BOOK TITLE	NOTES
108.		
109.		
110.		
111.		
112.		
113.		
114.		
115.		
116.		
117.		
118.		
119.		
120.		
121.		
122.		
123.		
124.		
125.		
126.		

SPECIAL GUEST STORY TIME!

Reader's name: _____

Relationship to you: _____

Date: _____ Location: _____

Reason for visit: _____
_____

We read these books together:

- _____ - _____
- _____ - _____
- _____ - _____

My favorite thing about reading with you is:
_____
_____

The book I liked reading to you the most was . . .
Title   Because
_____
_____
_____

Here are some reading suggestions from me to you: _____
_____
_____
_____

DATE	BOOK TITLE	NOTES
127.		
128.		
129.		
130.		
131.		
132.		
133.		
134.		
135.		
136.		
137.		
138.		
139.		
140.		

GO BIG!

Check out some chapter books that you can read together over the span of a few weeks. Your kiddo will look forward to picking up where you left off in the story. Bonus points if there are illustrations too!

DATE	BOOK TITLE	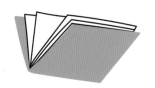	NOTES
141.			
142.			
143.			
144.			
145.			
146.			
147.			
148.			
149.			
150.			
151.			
152.			
153.			
154.			
155.			
156.			
157.			
158.			
159.			

DATE	BOOK TITLE	NOTES
160.		
161.		
162.		
163.		
164.		
165.		
166.		
167.		
168.		
169.		
170.		
171.		
172.		
173.		
174.		
175.		
176.		
177.		
178.		

Your personality is: _____

_____

Your favorite activities are: _____

_____

Reading with you is: _____

_____

The times of day that we read together are: _____

_____

You like books that are about or feature:

• _____ • _____

• _____ • _____

• _____ • _____

The book we return to again and again is:

_____

I think you like this book because: _____

_____

My favorite books to read to you are . . .

Title   *Because*

_____

_____

_____

DATE	BOOK TITLE	NOTES
179.		
180.		
181.		
182.		
183.		
184.		
185.		
186.		
187.		
188.		
189.		
190.		
191.		
192.		

BACK TO BOARD BOOKS

If you hung on to some of your child's favorite board books, bring them back out. The simple text and short sentences make great early-reader practice books.

DATE	BOOK TITLE		NOTES

193.
194.
195.
196.
197.
198.
199.
200.
201.
202.
203.
204.
205.
206.
207.
208.
209.
210.
211.

DATE	BOOK TITLE		NOTES
212.			
213.			
214.			
215.			
216.			
217.			
218.			
219.			
220.			
221.			
222.			
223.			
224.			
225.			
226.			
227.			
228.			
229.			
230.			

BOOKS TO GET YOU MOVING

Get those wiggles out!

Caribou Song by Tomson Highway, illustrated by John Rombough

Dancing Feet! by Lindsey Craig, illustrated by Marc Brown

Goal! by Mina Javaherbin, illustrated by A. G. Ford

I Got the Rhythm by Connie Schofield-Morrison,
illustrated by Frank Morrison

The Quickest Kid in Clarksville by Pat Zietlow
Miller, illustrated by Frank Morrison

BOOKS FOR RELAXING

And now, slow it down . . .

A Handful of Quiet: Happiness in Four Pebbles by
Thich Nhat Hanh, illustrated by Wietske Vriezen

Breathe like a Bear by Kira Willey, illustrated by Anni Betts

Gonna Move, Gotta Bounce, Have to Jumpity Jump!
by Jamaree Stokes, illustrated by Charli Vince

May All People and Pigs Be Happy by Micki
Fine Pavlicek, illustrated by John Pavlicek

You Are a Lion! And Other Fun Yoga Poses by Taeeun Yoo

DATE	BOOK TITLE		NOTES
231.			
232.			
233.			
234.			
235.			
236.			
237.			
238.			
239.			
240.			
241.			
242.			
243.			

TV TIE-INS

Pick up books about their favorite TV shows and movies. Or better yet, read the book before watching the movie! Your child will love seeing what was in their imagination on the big screen. Delving deeper into familiar worlds from the screen and vice versa can be inspiring. Plus, you might learn something too!

DATE	BOOK TITLE	NOTES
244.		
245.		
246.		
247.		
248.		
249.		
250.		
251.		
252.		
253.		
254.		
255.		
256.		
257.		
258.		
259.		
260.		
261.		
262.		

DATE	BOOK TITLE	NOTES
263.		
264.		
265.		
266.		
267.		
268.		
269.		
270.		
271.		
272.		
273.		
274.		
275.		
276.		
277.		
278.		
279.		
280.		
281.		

CHAPTER BOOKS TO READ TOGETHER

Reading big books will feel extra special.
Try these books and series together.

Brown Girl Dreaming by Jacqueline Woodson

Captain Underpants series by Dav Pilkey

Harry Potter: The Illustrated Collection by
J. K. Rowling, illustrated by Jim Kay

Prairie Lotus by Linda Sue Park

Sarai and the Meaning of Awesome by Sarai Gonzalez
and Monica Brown, illustrated by Christine Almeda

The Borrowers series by Mary Norton

The Dory Fantasmagory series by Abby Hanlon

The EllRay Jakes series by Sally Warner,
illustrated by Brian Biggs

The Jasmine Toguchi series by Debbi Michiko Florence

The Penderwicks series by Jeanne Birdsall

Time Quintet (*A Wrinkle in Time*) series by Madeleine L'Engle

Zoey and Sassafras series by Asia Citro,
illustrated by Marion Lindsay

SPECIAL GUEST STORY TIME!

Reader's name: _____

Relationship to you: _____

Date: _____ Location: _____

Reason for visit: _____
_____

We read these books together:

- _____ • _____
- _____ • _____
- _____ • _____

My favorite thing about reading with you is:
_____
_____

The book I liked reading to you the most was . . .

Title   *Because*
_____
_____
_____

Here are some reading suggestions from me to you: _____
_____
_____

DATE	BOOK TITLE	NOTES

282. _____
283. _____
284. _____
285. _____
286. _____
287. _____
288. _____
289. _____
290. _____
291. _____
292. _____
293. _____
294. _____
295. _____
296. _____
297. _____
298. _____
299. _____
300. _____

DATE	BOOK TITLE		NOTES

301.
302.
303.
304.
305.
306.
307.
308.
309.
310.
311.
312.
313.
314.
315.
316.
317.
318.
319.

DATE	BOOK TITLE	NOTES

320.
321.
322.
323.
324.
325.
326.
327.
328.
329.
330.
331.
332.
333.

DON'T STOP READING

Even if your budding student is starting to read on their own, don't stop reading together. Leveled reader books can be slow at this age, so the books you read together will keep them inspired, and the time together is just as valuable at five (or ten!) years old as it is at one.

BOOKS TO STRIVE FOR

Soon your youngster will be reading on their own
(still with a bit of help from you!). Here are some
books that they'll love to read when they're ready.

Anna Hibiscus series by Atinuke, illustrated by Lauren Tobia

Dog Man by Dav Pilkey

Encyclopedia Brown, Boy Detective by Donald J. Sobol

Junie B. Jones series by Barbara Park,
illustrated by Denise Brunkus

Lilly's Purple Plastic Purse by Kevin Henkes

Nya's Long Walk by Linda Sue Park, illustrated by Brian Pinkney

Priya Dreams of Marigolds & Masala by Meenal Patel

The Girl Who Loved Wild Horses by Paul Goble

The King of Kindergarten by Derrick Barnes,
illustrated by Vanessa Brantley-Newton

The Princess in Black series by Shannon
Hale, Dean Hale, and LeUyen Pham

The Undefeated by Kwame Alexander and Kadir Nelson

Under My Hijab by Hena Khan, illustrated by Aaliya Jaleel

DATE	BOOK TITLE	NOTES

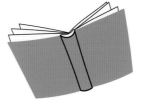

334.

335.

336.

337.

338.

339.

340.

341.

342.

343.

344.

345.

346.

347.

348.

349.

350.

351.

352.

DATE	BOOK TITLE	NOTES
353.		
354.		
355.		
356.		
357.		
358.		
359.		
360.		
361.		
362.		
363.		
364.		
365.		

WHAT WE'RE READING NEXT

Your personality is: _____

_____

Your favorite activities are: _____

_____

Reading with you is: _____

_____

The times of day that we read together are: _____

_____

You seem most interested in books that are about or feature:

- _____ - _____
- _____ - _____
- _____ - _____

The book we return to again and again is:

_____

I think you like this book because: _____

_____

My favorite books to read to you are . . .

Title	Because

INTERVIEW YOUR CHILD!

Ask your child these questions and write down their answers word for word!

What are some of your favorite books we've read this year? _____
_____
_____
_____

Why do you like them? _____
_____
_____
_____

If you were a character in a book, what character would you be?
What would the book be about? _____
_____
_____
_____

What's your favorite part about reading books with me? _____
_____
_____
_____

READING REFLECTIONS

Look back on the books you've logged this year and reflect on your time together. Then answer these questions:

The books we read the most were: _____
_____
_____
_____

I've noticed you grow in these ways during our reading time together: _____
_____
_____
_____

I'll cherish this memory from reading with you: _____
_____
_____
_____

Use this space to collect any other thoughts on your reading this year: _____
_____
_____
_____
_____
_____
_____
_____

YOU
DID IT!

Congratulations! If you wrote down even one book that you read each day, you've now read together more than 1,800 times. That's some serious quality time!

During your reading sessions, you've seen your child's focus sharpen, their interests expand, and their imagination blossom. You've seen them grow from processing simple concepts to complex thoughts. You've watched as they've developed empathy for characters and people they meet. And you've been by their side as they learned how to communicate, first nonverbally and now in whole paragraphs.

You've fostered their love of language, helped them learn about others and the world around them, and you've given them the most amazing gifts a parent can give a child: your time, full attention, and of course, your love.

At this point, your child is probably well on their way to learning how to read. As you continue your reading time together, you'll increasingly take turns with words and eventually whole books. In what seems like no time at all, your little bookworm will be reading independently.

In the next few pages, record your final reading reflections from these first five years with your child, then save this book as a keepsake to share with them when they're older.

HAPPY READING!

READING REFLECTIONS

Ask your child to draw a picture of you reading together in the space provided.

RESOURCES

WELL-READ CHECK-IN

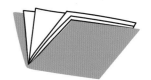

As you introduce your child to the world and the world of books, make sure you have an inclusive collection to read. Review your reading log periodically and ask yourself the following questions.

- Have we read books that portray characters of color, differently abled characters, or LGBTQ characters?
- If yes, have we read books that portray those characters as the main protagonists?
- Have we read books written or illustrated by people of color, people who identify as LGBTQ, or people from different cultures?

As your child grows, it's important to make sure that the books they read reflect the diversity of experience. For example, books about Black characters should show protagonists in a range of professions, locales, and hobbies. Books about girls should show them engaging in all types of sports and other pursuits.

Also think about the classics you might have grown up with, and evaluate whether they contain damaging stereotypes or images. If you share these with your child, think about how you'll talk to them about those stereotypes.

Source: Adapted from Lee & Low Books, "Checklist: 8 Steps to Creating a Diverse Book Collection."

MORE READING INSPIRATION

BRIGHTLY
https://www.readbrightly.com

Recommendations, tips, advice, and recorded story time for reading with children.

CALDECOTT MEDAL WINNERS
https://alsc-awards-shelf.org

Every year, the American Library Association awards the Caldecott to the artist of the "most distinguished American picture book for children."

#COLORMYSHELF ON SOCIAL MEDIA

Recommendations for diverse children's books.

COOPERATIVE CHILDREN'S BOOK CENTER
https://ccbc.education.wisc.edu/booklists

Run by the University of Wisconsin–Madison's School of Education, the CCBC provides a variety of reading lists filled with recommended books on a number of topics.

CORETTA SCOTT KING BOOK AWARDS
http://www.ala.org/rt/emiert/cskbookawards

These annual awards are presented to "outstanding African American authors and illustrators for children and young adults that demonstrate an appreciation of African American culture and universal human values."

LOCAL BOOKSTORES AND LIBRARIES

Just browsing at your local bookstore or library can unearth a wealth of new titles for you and your little one. Plus, you get a fun book-centered outing together. Check out your local bookstore or library, or search for independent bookstores at https://www.indiebound.org.

SCHOLASTIC BOOK LISTS BY AGE
https://www.scholastic.com/parents/books-and-reading/books-and-reading -guides/recommended-childrens-books-by-age.html

Scholastic offers lots of different lists and suggestions for your early reader, sorted by age and topic so you can follow your little one's passion and interests.

ABOUT THE AUTHOR

L. J. TRACOSAS writes books for curious kids and edits anything she can get her hands on. She's published more than ten books for young readers, including the bestselling Sink Your Teeth Into series, as well as licensed titles with Mattel, WWE, and others. L. J. lives in Atlanta with her husband, son, and too many cats. She makes books in memory of her son Miles.